(SOLVE FOR) X

TURTLE POINT PRESS   BROOKLYN, NEW YORK

KATHARINE COLES　　(SOLVE FOR) X

Requests for permissions to make copies of any part of the work should be sent to:
Turtle Point Press, 208 Java Street, Fifth Floor, Brooklyn, NY, 11222
info@turtlepointpress.com

Library of Congress Catalogue-in-Publication Data
Names: Coles, Katharine, author.
Title: (Solve for) X / Katharine Coles.
Description: First edition. | Brooklyn, New York : Turtle Point Press, [2022]
Identifiers: LCCN 2021040969 | ISBN 9781933527598 (trade paperback)
Subjects: LCGFT: Poetry.
Classification: LCC PS3553.047455 S65 2022 | DDC 811/.54—dc23
LC record available at https://lccn.loc.gov/2021040969

Book design by Crisis

ISBN 978-1-933527-59-8

Printed in the United States of America

First Edition

FOR HELEN MULDER,
MY FIRST POETRY TEACHER,
WHO TAUGHT ME
NOT TO FEAR BEAUTY,

AND FOR
KATHRYN BOND STOCKTON,
WHO FIRST TAUGHT ME
TO LOVE AMBIGUITIES.

CONTENTS

(SOLVE FOR) X

ACCURACY

If the sky is falling
Hunt meteors or raise

Your umbrella; keep
Your head down, take cover, this

Gets worse. In your nit-
Picky life, you only ever

Wanted mountains' endless
Flaming, a yellow eye.

Once I learned it's wrong to be moved
By one's own words, I stopped. Of course,
We all should leave off weeping and consider
The past dispassionately, in order

That we might make a coherent
Picture, or at least keep some corner of it
Intact. I remember my brother's boyhood
Cruelties, for example, he only mine.

We use them to fuel present grievance,
Which is nonsense, but both of us recall groves
Of inexplicable trees, so maybe they or the fires

We remember taking them occurred. Shed
Tears for their passing if you want. Meantime, what
About the future, hmm? What about it?

ANOTHER DISASTER

Call me ice-
Hearted bitch. Mean-
Time everything flies
Apart, blaze

And shrapnel, stars
Black-holing and roofs
Falling in. Always
The electric cuts

Out and the tap's endless
Dripping, and he's
Still looking for a Band-aid.

We don't have time for
This, I say. Said
We never did.

AUBADE

Rhyme *trough* with *itself.*
Keep denying the existence of things
You can't see. *Rummage* and *derange,*
Try *orange* with *forage* for the sheer hell

Of almost. Everywhere dark is all
And nothing at all, though I feel him
Breathing through me, the warm
Soft in and out of him, *inhale*

A word for falling into some
Dizzy interior. Listen, I could
Almost hear my own arrival
Breathless into the world, a *come*

The world composes out of un-
Knowable good. Come morning.

BODY

New catastrophe, same
Old, *this* one's atoms
Reconfigure, genes profligate,
Prone to undoing. Face it,

I am who I am. Do you
Think you're one trick
At a time, then what? Specific
Less-than-minor planet fastened to

Gravity, every solar system
Fills gorgeous space it makes
Itself. Oh, boy. Look:

The more you expand, you
Think that hiccup in you spits
Out error, replicating blue.

CENTO CONSIDERING LIFE AND AFTERLIFE
(INCLUDING A LINE FROM FRANK O'HARA)

It has been a bad decade for God.
To begin with, we are losing women.
There is no formula for this.
If nothing else, it is a puzzle.

Think, for example, about the experience
Of intense nausea. You are in the grip of it.
Stay standing, I tell myself,
Spinning like a fluid in a centrifuge.

This is the famous problem of evil.
In the final out there, my body maintains
Its gravitational bearings. We should be careful
Not to draw overarching conclusions.

The elderly are more curious about hell.
Mine is as good as it gets, albeit with pink drinks.
My mother set out little vases of cigarettes.
There was raucous cheering and calculated yelling.

That seems a lifetime ago. I ended up
Observing the spinning constellation.
We should all be so lucky. Many people
Were curious about what that meant.

Jesus does not get the most
Attention. Some religious people
Have asked, When does he sleep? And,
Impossible, right? This is hardly definitive proof

You will find calm amid the chaos,
The provisional way of things now. *Grace
to be born and live as variously as possible.*
Things get really interesting when we look.

Warm before you
Touch, containment so clear
And entire you gaze

Through it, brought down
To size. Your palm-
Self, reduced, creases

And deepens, as if knowing
Your future could let you
Understand it.

CURIO

The penis is the miniature of the man, ergo
Death's head lies beneath skin fallen
Away—so this figure shows
Its logic, impeccably forged

And wrought in silver. When have I seen
Such a delicious blaze, body no longer
Naked in the flesh but rather
Out of it. This one I fail

To photograph but remember among
Skeletons twined with serpents
Winding orifices and sockets, the skull
Peering out behind a face un-

Suspecting of the grin beneath
That curious, oh-so-serious mouth.

Not fossil not decay unfurls
A shining ladder and makes

Rescue all. In movies
Lets fall, tears off

The specs and love
Follows. Years since

I lay in a bed of my own
Making, my skull

Once shorn its own
Assertion dreaming

Impossible billow
And waft. So many

Years with someone
Touching me I could

Not sleep until
Last night your hand

Cupped my head, found
Its kind of falling.

1. Weigh every word.
Books piled, head

Perfectly still, every
Spine transports

Explosions, some
Intentional, others

Grand. Accident carries
Precedent: proper female

Posture never will be
A head posing

2. Questions. What
Composes and does

Self impose
Itself? Balanced

In closing, the books
Ignite inside, they fizz

And spark and send
Up flares. What im-

Position. Damage
Done: almost none.

DISORDER

I will be dust again
The book tells me

And will be fine. All
One can do: pulling

Herself together, why
-ever she ought to.

Don't you get tired
Composing a self: gloves, hat,

Tiny buttons? I'm even
Tired of romance proposing

Its endless line. I'd refuse
Sequins to release you, but

Spare me glued-down
Bows and kitten heels. Give

Me altitude. I want
The world to see me

Curse in public. I want
The curse to stick.

DOG TAG

Smaller than my dog
And differently proportioned

I stalked the west side.
My coat, like his, was black.

Back then, if you wanted
To pacify a man

You had to let him touch you.
Some parts stay the same. Mostly

I declined, thinking
That's what power smells like,

Who needs it? The dog agreed.
In truth, he outweighed me

By a good fifty percent.
Passersby mistook him,

Jumping at their own shadows.
His wagging helped nothing.

Of course, I sympathized,
But what else could I tell him?

15

Full of hands, the world
Offered a body to touch, but

People lowered their eyes
And sidled slowly by.

EQUINOX

Think of words I have
Promised, I've withheld. How

They balance, blossoms
Pushing forth then falling

When the last freeze comes
Too late. Year after year

This day finds me full
Of myself and frolic. Too late,

The mantra I don't know
I should speak until it is.

Take up all the air. Not you,
Of course, my friend, my beloved,
Nor any of your numerous
Innocent acquaintances, of whom

I'm bound to take care, each
An exception to the rule and me
Only a woman who thus
Takes you in hand. If not me,

Who? What I say includes
Every man, even when I mean
No-one, no one man, a woman
As if I ever do. All these words

Are masculine, every one. Go on,
Have them. Make them about you.

FINE DINING

Totting up exes with an old friend
Over a dinner we can afford now,
Accounting things we used to take for granted
And thought were normal and continuous

Like how I've always fainted with a fever, or when
Suddenly standing up, or falling little deathlike into
That delicious and complete evacuation
I thought took everyone the same

Until much later. Nobody spoke of it.
I admit, this is an older woman's poem,
Though really not much changes: you learn
To keep your feet under you no matter what

Even when your tights have bound your ankles
And your back is shoved against the wall.

If you can do nothing for me
I can't do for myself, why bother?

Silhouetted against the window's
Moonlight, you loom and range,

A sleeping mountain. What could
You want, my darling, now I lie

Pinned to the mattress, wondering
What on earth could move me.

I always wanted to be somewhere
Or never. Always wanted the

Freedom of one thing

And others. What about
The rose, I always said, an

Emblem of itself, the apple

We love not because it
Fruits but for its stick

-ing points. In

Some seasons, the rose, as in the
Blossom, opens its throat.

Get me on with it. Get me a fork, whisky and branch, a float in my own downriver parade. Drift me under a string of bridges, through cricks and bends; wave me past the *et-tu?* and the *yes, me too*, on water, always singing.

I'll feed you a line. You feed me a longer one.

Then let's both swallow.

He's about to become
All about light. Limning
And glittering in its way. Not

The subject, the self
Bearded in its dignity,
But the sun setting

Trees on fire behind him
So, like us, he's lost in woods
He envisions. Are they

Inside him? Paint
Itself reflecting. What
Do we choose to see?

Put down shadow,
Dapple, the world we keep
Thinking we can know.

We wouldn't wear each other's clothes. She
Would grow beyond me, like the rest,
And bootstrap herself to heaven. My sister
Would overlook me. She would loft opinions
With no evidence, they would spin
And hang in air, nothing to be done.
My sister if I had one would appear

Nothing like me, only better, more
Golden and broad beamed, more put
Out, with the kind of lips that,
You know. My sister would adjust
Her bosom and head into any fray
While I'd recede into the distance. I
Would, as always, stay away.

IF MY DREAMS ABOUT FLYING
ARE REALLY ABOUT SEX

I want to stay up here
As long as I can, surveying

Hills and farmland, tall
buildings, avenues leading

Where I like, wondering
What dreams about sex

Are about. I want
This body to buoy me

Forever, full of bubbles and air,
Though, frankly, I've never

Landed this gizmo before,
And I don't know how.

The future becomes

My mistake. I am never on time
For anything, but now

I have an excuse, which

I also have no use for, given
My oddly on-

Time reputation. Maybe everyone

Follows the clock
I'm on, tick and tock

Little deaths we all work

Hard ignoring. Maybe I
Wish we all had more

Sense, if not better.

Develop a personal relationship with

An idea, soft and hairless or muscled

Over. It scars and frays

On its own, skull

Niched for brain and eyes lamping

Your way; ribs caging the heart

Murmuring as if

You might forget it, stitched

Together by tissue raveling

Time which sings you

Asleep, chatters

All night. No matter. Teeth

Unscrew before you finish

Chewing, spine unfastens though

You still need its carriage. Rattled

As if you ever were

Together, not

Open for tongues

Parsing syllables. Mark

The place to remember

What have you

Hidden too well.

1. What we owned before
We tossed it. What lightens
The vessel sailing where
We wish, remaining

Blithe in going. Being
What we let go on purpose,
Now that it no longer serves
Our needs. Unlike *lagan*

Jetsam also floats, floating
The point: if we choose
Not to keep it, why not send it

Wherever, and save our
-selves? Watch the horizon why not,
Wafting toward it, going over there.

2. Not *flotsam*, then, not what
Sinks then rises again to haunt
Us. Not what we lose by capsize

Being wreckage. Don't
Call it misadventure, to plunge
Deep into dark sounding

Then release goodies in pieces
Back to surface, keeping
What isn't buoyant

Enough to float. Not a body,
Then, which will. Thinking
Glisters. Thinking *hold*.

3. Not derelict, either,
As in *sunk, just gone*

Or *beyond recovery*, as in
My voice, its song. All that's left

I warble. The waters sing
So long, so long.

First, squirrels, calling
Annoyance at my progress
To fetch the paper, my news
All their concern, none of it.

Then, the hummingbirds
Rocketing straight up
And topping the trees,
Scouting for feeders I am late

Hanging on the balcony,
Buzzing my ears. Where
Have I been, the orioles
Also insist, or rather

Where is their grape jelly
And could I go away now?
Every day passes through
Demand and response, raccoon

Growling over the bins, food
Herself for the rarely spotted
Bobcat easing his shy
Body up the walk, curving

Himself to see me. Even
After dark I hear the eerie *Who
Are you*, wings with and without
Feathers filling the air

With audible silence. Some
Questions have no answers
I can give. Others
None I will take.

In my friend's mind, a pond
Or lake, too big to tell at night, stretches

Rocky beach to rushes. It lies under
Stars and moonlight, reflecting
Both, absorbing neither, and hides

What it contains, which may be
Or not. My father's mind

Also brims over, sometimes
Smooth, sometimes ruffled. As
Does mine. Maybe something happens,

Maybe it didn't. I can't say for sure
The lake means memory or its loss,

Gerda's or my father's, only
It laps coolly at the dark,
It ebbs and flows with light.

But not of it—saying
The world is too much. With us

It's always one thing
Or another. Both if I could

Sleep and could not
The young hawk isn't far

Enough fledged to stop
Shrilling for mother

Who lets it fly farther
Every day until at last

It breaks the spiral
Then will be cloud

Ruffling the grass
A wide and distant call.

Out of the cartoon jumble
Wish; from wish an end

We long for. We think we see clear
Past it, though forestalled again

It gentles us, its shock
Expected. Still, we can

Imagine ourselves back
Out once more, could turn

Time on its head. The past
Believes in itself, persists

While presence fails. As will
The future, when it comes to call.

MISHEARD

Say you're interested in pig satisfaction, I thought
You said, but you said *pay*. Love,

I hear around the matter's edges into a heart
The world sharpens and dissolves.

My doctor runs his tests but it's nothing
Material, nothing gone

Wrong down my ears' intricate spiral
So the problem's all

In my head. It mutters and I'm
Misled. Does it

Matter I'm so divided I can't
Hear you?

MISSING

The building between the buildings. A child,
Graveyards. That woman's mind
Searches pews, putting her heart in it,
Her husband holding his hands where

Her faith lies. Under our feet, another
Pile of rubble. Written over,
She raises her eyes to find
A vaulted ceiling, a gesture

Beyond. The latest old columns stand
but the windows cast white
Light over everything, every pane
Blown where once played crimson

And blue across the stones. Look.
Cold-eyed, they look back.

People are never who we believe.
Why should they be? Especially
When she wields future angles
And gorgeous silver hair. Imagine,

Thirty years on, for example, you
Trailing intellect and charm, real
As the future, so don't let her kid
You. Her evident interest, her side-

Cocked head: she might even be
Listening
                    and all that. Meanwhile,
Here in the real, you never will
Escape. If not her, someone

Always remembers what you ate,
Exactly where you sit.

MOTE

Fly in a dry wind
Or be brought down by rain;
Drift on a shelf, dimming
The gleam of wood and polish.

Suspend a beam of light
And please the eye
Not watching for the eye
But only your own freedom,

Wafting beyond care
Or simple obligation
So small at last
You only seem to vanish.

I am, then I am. Can appear
And can ghost. Won't occur
Naturally. Could be open
And shut, be mistaken or have

A high dynamic range. Sensitive
Or not, I may take on
Many positions at once,
My shadow crushed, negative

Shining through, face blurred
Into. How many expressions
Should I keep? How many shots
Can I give you and not

Have to shoot you? I wasn't
Always exposed, or even present.

I never had a sister, but if I did
She carried waist

-level like a clutch, hand loose,
Her finger ready to move the trigger

A hair, needs must. If her gun
Needed to move her hand

Was all over it. In her hand, the gun
I find myself missing.

Unless I grow green leaves
And scatter perfume and petals
I must remain myself,
Stuck in my body. Time

Scatters perfume, and stars
Cover the earth at midnight.
Stuck in a body, in time
I might become something.

Dawn recovers the earth,
Telling the same old story:
Everyone turns into something.
Can't someone else shoulder

This same-told history?
It's always the woman looking
Over her shoulder, some man
Chasing her past herself.

Looking back, she only
Slows herself down. The sun
Chases her past her present, into
Time she must outrun.

Slow down. Even a god
Can't chase what won't flee.
Tempus fugit. Don't run.
Turn here, put your foot down.

Time can't chase if I won't fly.
I can't become myself
Until I put my roots down,
Unless I grow green leaves.

They always come free, the old masters,
Though we're centuries out of pocket.
The women we pay to see.

For the masters, we've already paid in
Money, bodies, history. Still, we say
Always, old masters work free.

Shoot panties from a cannon's mouth
Like comets. Mask up, superwoman.
The women we pay to see

Fade, behind bars. We've paid
Lives for secrets and taken our change.
Always free, the old masters came,

Always in season, flaneuring
The boulevard, solicitous, soliciting
The women they pay to see

And to paint, not to mention
What they exert on the side. In time,
They always come, the old masters. Free

And gay, the women mask
Desire with paint. Some
Women they pay. To see

Their labor, I proffer my cash,
Consent. In the official museum,
They come free, the old masters. Always,
These women I pay to see.

Is hypothesis a moving target. Do we
Remake what we ask
With what we know. Can we
Begin with a question and also

End with a question, and is it
The same or a new one
And if we are wrong do we ask again
Until we forget we always started

Awry. Is it our nature,
Being wrong, and so do we err
Out of mistakenness or pleasure,
Broken selves or fire. Where

In the end will we find our answers.
Tell me will we still be there.

NEIGHBORS

When the roof blew away
They flew right out. In disarray, though

Don't think what that means. Think

Kitchen, think ladle in the pot, soup
Rolling over. Think

Flame lying in the pipe, not yet

Breathing, a blue idea
Gathering itself. The hand

Grasping the knob, ready to turn.

NO REASON

beyond art

Turning another page, staying up late
And unsupervised so far

Into maturity. Like all women,

I'm told, I aspire to a certain stability
And may have believed it would be

Supplied by heavy ballast, say

Marble, though we've all been given
The pedestal warning and taken heed.

Taken head, I might rather say, and strong.

Maybe an anchor would be better. Forgetting
An anchor hooks by chain to something

Equally heavy. A battleship. A heart.

There's no point sitting
Around, tomorrow being
Never a sure thing. Truth is

We were made for the future's
Perpetual reach, endless
Calculations. In which moment

Would you have me
Exercise patience?
I'd rather put it off.

It matters only what time it is
My ticker keeps, jolting me
Awake all night with its green strobe.

Think of it as a pulsar pumping
Light. Think of it, if you do, as my all
-in-all. I always say, I'm eating

My heart out. I've given up
Needing to know what else
It means. I say, It beats me.

OPTICS

If you want to see everything
You need other eyes, turned
Not inward like mine
But outward, not one

But many. If a fly sees me
Coming in all directions, looking
Like that makes everything
Happen fast. See a glimmer through

The lens inside your eye
Or outside, the one you hang on
Your nose or lower your face to. Tell

Me, do stars blind my eyes or only
Your own, mirage in
Which you lose yourself.

The mind likes to think the mind
Chats with itself, amusing

Outside-in. In this
It resembles the heart, no more

In order, I hate to say, no less
Reflexive. It's the way a man's organ

Has been said to lead him around
By the nose, as it were. Said by men,

Mind, not me. If you believe reports,
Like him all I can do is follow.

PANTOUM AT TWILIGHT

Because our windows look like sky
Outside, you can't see in—only
Light reflecting blue, streaked white,
Only leaves flashing

Outside. You can't see in, only
That there is an inside, not
Only leaves flashing
But among them a shadow showing

Inside. There is not
A body but a haunting, surfaces
And among them a shadow. I'll show you
If you bring your eyes closer

A body haunting the surfaces
Of table and shelf, a curve of chair.
Bring your eyes closer:
There, sitting and reading, a man

Curves the chair. Table and shelf
Emerge as the sun sets here;
There, sitting and reading, the man
Turns on the light and suddenly

Emerges. Out here, the sun sets,
Light reflecting blue, streaked with red,
The light turning on us because
Suddenly the window looks like sky.

To bed, far away and without you, I take devices: phone, open laptop, e-reader. Facebook tracks me in time.

E-reader. Facetime. Laptop, open to Facebook: watch, I'm screening my dreams in time.

One glass of water, one wine. I shut the lights. Can I face my screen of dreams in time?

Until lights-off, I hoard the pillows. Pour one glass of water, one wine. There's enough for another.

Alone, I take all the pillows.

I swear, I take no lover.

Turn off your surveillance. I've disabled my devices. In my distance, so far, I'm up to nothing in bed.

PERIODIC

Planetary, how
We're always being turned, when

A star might have
Its own spin on things.

The perfect posthumous brain
Slices elegantly. Never

Falls apart. Sleeps
When it should and holds onto

What it knows. It shows
Signs of insanity or genius

Lobe by swollen lobe, not who
It loved or anything

Material. So I am
Two legs, two eyes, one

Mind and heart counting a-one-
And-a-two and at last

Won't be counted.

POWER

I look but I find no battle between the sexes,
just a bit of a struggle to see who gets to do what.
—Frederick Seidel

Power is when no one comments on
The nightmare that is your body
At your sex and age, your body *given*
Until you expose yourself—please

Don't make me
Imagine. Strip off: I'll have to go
Head-to-head with you, fillup
To shank, wild hair to skin flap

To fatty lump. Explicit:
Hate anyone's body, hate
Your own, so slack you wouldn't
Know where to put it or what

Do with it or how
To make it please you.

QUARREL

Like you, wasn't I told
Not to. Sit tight,

Wait, I was also
Told, so I did. As

You are, I always say,
Not as you were,

Though one, I hear,
Leads to the other.

QUESTIONS

                    All I have
Anymore: nonsense,

More nonsense. I never know

One from the other, thinking
How thinking makes me

Feel. One is one thing

And another is also
One thing, and in each

Happily I abide.

When I was young, I was too busy
To be angry, and now I'm not.
In spite of everything, I have
Less time than ever for that. Despite

We're all vanishing, I admit
The world can rub the wrong way
As often as never. Only, don't lift
The lid off. Only lilacs waft

Swoony perfume all over
The greening, and orioles
Flash extravagant orange selves
Where leaves burgeon. All the world's

Problems. And these. What more
Could anyone, even me, desire?

Flowers not a garden, flowers strewn
And spread without a plot. The garden
Fills with flowers, garden not
A garden, tangle of bramble wilderness

And berry, limb and stem. How much bliss
Can a person take, how long? What
Green and petal, what aromas
Spicing the afternoon? When we came here

I didn't want a garden, couldn't have cared
Less for flowers, I thought. In this welter
Of what we've placed and what flies in

Like magic on the wind, I stand and raise
My nose to breezes smelling green
As soil, arriving here, from here.

SEDUCTION

No-one looks at my arms any more
And says roll up those sleeves, I must
Use my tongue to follow one thing
To another and would you show me your

What-have-you. This is good however
Long it's been because maybe I was
Once too willing to say, whatever,
Sure, if you think so. Which between us

Generated mostly boredom &c
And so has almost never been the best
Answer, though it's also brought I confess
A few (not enough, in balance) interesting

If not always entirely satisfying
Moments in the short run.

It was like climbing a mountain to those of us who'd climbed one. To the others, it was like, I suppose, something else. In other words, we let everybody find her own figure of speech.

Not that it—speech—lay thick on the ground, or mountain; it presented itself one word at a time, far between. A body had to keep an eye out, like for firewood at dusk, or else

miss her chance. Nobody else, let's face it, cared about metaphor, or even simile, the like-it-or-not-ness of the mountain pretty much getting between a body and her musing, in its going. One

step at a time, anyone could lose herself or someone else just staring at her feet. And *if a body meet a body* is not mere speech but something that could happen, like hopping a bus—though on the mountain

you'll catch no rides, worse luck, the mountain requires to be climbed on foot, one after the other, nothing else will get you up it. There's nothing like such obduracy but in the wild, nobody
can tell you otherwise. No simple figure,

this struggle: just a crag, your burden, and your own two feet. Say otherwise, talk through your hat, which I don't care for.

Easy enough for you to take
An attitude if you have no tendons

Requiring to be warmed up, those
Little gestures we make, asking

The body, will you now? Only an expert
Can tell if the skeletons are male

Or female: let's guess male
In reality, female in imagination

Where the grotesque
And frightening take their time.

No time to obey. This one
A tiny bit cracked, this
One intact, going
Strong. Made to bear

Or break, made to wall
Us in enough, lest
They become too much
Even for us to take

Who made them. I
Remember the straight
Edge I tried to follow where

It went. How my pencil
Went its own way,
Astray.

SOMEDAY

                    one will heft
The other body gone
Limp, evacuated, beside
Ourselves. Not now not yet

One of us will hold an
-other hand in lamplight, head
Cocked, listening for what
Comes. We have pamphlets

And instructions, advice
We need to rise
Though dawn withholds long
As it will. *Hard winter.* Go down

-stairs to the kitchen.
Light the house and wait.

To enchant you, I must be different from you. You decide how. Decide normal is what you are, so where difference lies I need to keep enchantment's lovely engine revved, sitting still, hum-humming away. Say *there*. Or say I never sit but wander, errant, murmuring, *Sure, I'll be all that*, so you never notice.

And you for me? If I'm true north, you too will find your-self

The space where difference lies. What happens then?

SPRING

Could spend all my time grassing
That way. Or this: could read
Novels, all of them, find happiness

Between flights I dream here
And there, wheels up, eyes
Pointed skyward. Where
Is there not the world

To be found: today greening
And spiced with hyacinths
I can smell all the way up
Where I keep my nose

Under my hat, where sorrow
Also blossoms, unlooked for
And sudden at my feet.

goddamit, Father said, *Don't*
Horse about, and *Time to get*

Serious, but never
Don't sleep around,

As if he meant, *Don't*
Fritter your life

Anywhere. He didn't
Want me to die without

What he wanted or
Not to have made myself

Into—what? He worried
I might become, who

Knows, haunted by stuff
Nobody could see. Wave

Goodbye, goodbye
Best chance. I wonder if he

Found what he wanted, looked
It in the eye, and chose.

UNDONE

Stop solving. The perfect
Lives somewhere else. Here

Fall eats its way across the foothills,
Not cold yet, burning

The way the world tells me
Time is coming, red and cold

And fierce. On the other side,
The opposite. Shadows shrinking

And a sky so huge
I can't look it in the eye.

I want you only when you aren't there: not heart but heart-beat, darkened core of me.

I want to want but not to want you only. I want not to have you, or I might.

Not heart but heartbeat wanting its idea: *I want you only if you're never coming.*

Knowing my heart—not muscle, but its song—what would you touch?

Say, *I want you only*

Heartless. Take my pulse.

VIRTUE

I remember all it once
Obliged, the what-now of it,

Only for example. In youth
I never had much use for properties

Flagged by men, though yes, practice
Makes perfect, and so on, and will

Be on the test. In passing
You may verge, you may

Impose your truth on others
And so become yourself.

Stop acting
Surprised. Stop
Believing you might be

An exception. Your
System was only

Ever a Rube Goldberg
Machine, geared up, glee
-ful, going nowhere. So

You haven't actually
Hurt anyone—have you?—

Doesn't make you
A good one or let you
Wag yourself about, like

Virtue, *Show*
Me. Make me

A carnival ride, my
High horse; donate
Your sweet meats

To the food bank. *Glug,*
Glug, so much to do. Let

Me decide. Make yourself
Useful, withdraw. I can
Cut you off, and I will.

One belongs to her heart, one
Her kidneys. One germinated

Children, the other bore. Give
A simple explanation, as if

The body could be. Say
She is herself and her own

Lost twin absorbed
In muscle and sinew deep

As a needle winkling
Its lone eye. Window or mirror:

Come in, get lost, the same
Flip of the fingers. The woman I knew

Mouthed words or handed,
Whichever, could make you

Understand her over wind
Or in the dark, which, she once touched

Me, is the longest thing. As,
Her other mouth said, is the light.

WOMEN WITH FLYING HEADS

I know, it's normal, a woman shooting
Things off, especially the bits most

Prone to being not where you
Put them for keeping. Don't ask, where's

Her head at and when did she lose it?
Remember to watch for shrapnel

And unexploded ordnance strewn
Round the garden. Also,

Her second most volatile
Part can go off *in situ*, no less

Frightening but at least a man
Can keep it in hand. Maybe,

Though, the right questions
Are, Why wouldn't heads roll,

Under the circumstances? And,
How good would that feel?

What it means about a woman she wouldn't
Or says so. Her sly smile

Inverted, her reveal. Is she the type
Who composes, who begins

Her skin care regime every year
The day before summer expecting

Vavoom? She lays down
Poison, can't abide the long

Revving of bees in the lavender,
Draws her veil over small windows

Asking to be looked through, not seen.

(SOLVE FOR) X

We can lay that to rest,
You already turning

Him into one thing, me
Another we can describe

Simply:
He was. Mums

For November end
Everything until

It begins
Flying apart, scraps

And numbers, secrets
Ordinary, black and white. So

He never was
What anyone thought. So

He is un-
Doing, schrapping out

Sparks and bits of metal. Why
Our own privacies

Held so close are we
Surprised? We thought

We loved we didn't
Know. Turning,

They told us
Children, Death is only

The beginning. Never
Was. Even then.

We all began in the dark
I'm told, though I like to think

I drifted in milky lumin
-escence, intact as a balloon,

As gassy and light. I saved
My breath for later, when

I'd need it to double
Down, no other variable

Coming to make me
Change sides. I like thinking

My body knew what it was
About from the start, busy being

Itself—why split hairs—even
Then wanting no spare

Baubles to take out and show,
Nothing to waggle at you

Beyond my own digits. Why
Complicate things, why put in

All that extra effort? I had,
I learned in time, enough

Fingers and toes to count
10 then 20 in so many

Beats of a nearly
Symmetrical heart. Two eyes,

Identical as may be, two
Hands, two breasts I bore

Before me, not even
Thinking how they had become

Wanted, become mine to offer
Or withhold as I wished

With all my other secrets
Tucked up inside, safe

And magical, my own
I was born believing.

If a word contains both time and how
We pass it, telling over moments
The way we turn beads
To prayer, for you I want

Only more of all of it: desire,
Ways to spend it. At last, your body
Wrung out, I wish for you sleep
And no end, a dream that growls

And flickers pleasure down
Your nerves. Be nimble, be quick—
Listen: what you make
is yours when you open your hand

And then, who knows
What happens? Everything goes.

Will never need
His beauty or know

What he would be
Without it. His eyes
Look back from such

Standing, so true
The shoulders from which

He dangles his body
It could leave you off
Your head. But he sits

And sinks into himself
As if he could go

Incognito, in-
Visible in his self
-made camouflage.

never made the world good
Or time less odd, some

Indivisible number hitching
Off into infinity. How could

Anything be stranger
Than day as it opens

Itself before my eyes
This morning: to the east

Clouds swaddling the mountains,
West a lake reflecting

Blue sky coming. Always
New weather, and I

Can only ever watch
This moment hovering overhead

And the horizon, telling me
All I need to know.

Too dazzled to land and bug
-eyed, the fly just circles, abuzz.

The horse shimmies her stripes
And keeps eating. What keeps

A zebra happily inside
Such an outrageous skin? Hidden

In plain view, I always say,
Only one place to be.

Unwieldy-hearted, browsing the blue, I never
Imagine looming. Draw my shadow
Self behind, cast down, a figure
Dimming waves, fields, the shining

Pinnacled cities. Send people
Netherward, from up here too tiny to be
Thought of, heads upturning
When the windows tremble. What a

Distance to travel, pulse and froth
Rumbling the air, chewing, bearing smaller
Spheres, like anyone armed to tumble forth
Into gravity. So relieved, my gondola

Lofts beneath its gassy envelope, my breath
Held. A spark will set me off.

Pace grey parrots, most birds don't
Do it, though a bee accomplishes mind-
Quirk of absence. Quiz her with dots:
A bee hums quantity-wards, if not

Every time getting there, better
Than random. How home
In, if you can't tell some-

Thing from aught, buzz-zoom
Winging from what void over-
Takes the center? Toddlers

Don't get—some grown humans
Never come to grips with—emp-
ty sky overtaking, all
Field, nothing to count within.

ZZZZ

She doesn't want to harm me, so
She hums. She prefers living alone,
Needing a single twig, just one
Hole. Like me she likes browsing

The desert where a breeze wafts
Her dry, where she dozes
On sand and ephemerals
Astonish by the thousands,

Brilliant and willing when the brief
Rains wake them. Out here, a female
Can do it all on her own
Time, and will, and goes on

Choosing, sounding herself entire,
One bare horizon to another.

NOTES

Page 5: After Guy Claxton: Radio West, July 1, 2016. https://radiowest.kuer
.org/post/intelligence-flesh-1

Page 6: *New York Times*, September 20, 2015. "Googling for God," Seth
Stephens-Davidowitz. "Why I Use Trigger Warnings," Kate Manne. "A
Toxic Work World," Anne-Marie Slaughter. "How Federer Thrives in
an Age of Disruption," Gerald Marzorati. "Brain Tumor as Zen Master,"
Adrienne Brodeur.

Page 9: Cabinet of Curiosities, ME Collector's Room, Berlin. For Lance and
Andi Olsen.

Page 11: Paul Strand, *Anna Attinga Frafra, Accra, Ghana*. Picture of a teenage
girl balancing books on her head.

Page 19: For Kay.

Page 21: "Here's the thing about an apple: it sticks in the throat." Richard
Powers

Page 22: "On a branch / floating downriver / a cricket, singing." Issa, trans-
lated by Jane Hirschfield

Page 24: This specific painting does not exist.

Page 30: For definitions, I relied on the Wikipedia page on jetsam.

Page 35: For Gerda Saunders and Bill Coles.

Page 42: Some of the terms manipulated in this poem were taken from
Wikipedia pages on exposure, autobracketing, chrome key, and sandwich
printing.

Page 43: From a sentence by Rachel Kushner.

Page 46: Among the art works referenced in this poem are G-Force Drive,
E. V. Day; Victoria's Secret, Robin Kahn; and Superwoman, Kiki Kogelnik.

Page 51: After a line by Michael Malone.

Page 60: With thanks to Julian Stannard.

Page 67: "Squelettes dans des attitudes acrobatiques," Kawanabe Kyosai, 1881. *Ghosts and Hells: the Underworld in Asian Art*, Musée du quai Branly, Paris, 2018.

Page 72: *Poor horse. It was leap and die or live and be haunted by the ability to choose.* —Peter Heller

Page 79: Hokusai and others on "de femmes a tetes volantes ou 'au long cou." *Ghosts and Hells: the Underworld in Asian Art*, Musée du quai Branly, Paris, 2018.

Page 88: *New York Times* "Sketchbook," 2/26/19.

Page 90: Math Bee: Honeybees Seem to Understand the Notion of Zero; National Public Radio Weekend Edition Sunday, aired June 10th, 2018.

ACKNOWLEDGMENTS

Poems from this collection have appeared in the following journals and magazines:

Axon: "Seduction," "History of Painting, Part X,"
"Undone" (as "Toward Winter")

Battery Journal: "Pantoum in Prose," "Villanelle in Prose,"
"Sonnet in Prose," "Zeppelin," "Zzzzz"

DIAGRAM: "If Dreams About Flying Are Really
About Sex," "Another Country," "Multiple Exposure"

Gulf Coast: "Dead Matter"

Hudson Review: "Curio"

Image: "*My body steps into history, imagine*," "Cento Considering
Life and Afterlife (Including a Line from Frank O'Hara"

Ocean State Review: "(solve for) X," "Pantoum at Twilight," "If I Had a Sister"

Poetry: "Sestina in Prose"

Poetry Northwest: "Missing," "Another Disaster" (reprint)

Scoundrel Time: "Women with Flying Heads," "Another Disaster"

Seneca Review: "Neighbors," "Sonnet in Prose," "Seven Poses"

Sugarhouse Review: "Think"

Terrain.org: "Zzzzz," "Zeppelin"

Seven poems from the collection were included in the anthology *Abstractions* from Recent Work Press in Canberra, Australia: "National Museum of Women in the Arts," "Accuracy," "Deportment," "Dog Tag," "Mother Poem," "Organ Recital," "No Reason."

"*My body steps into history, imagine*," was included in the anthology *Metamorphoses* from Recent Work Press in Canberra, Australia.